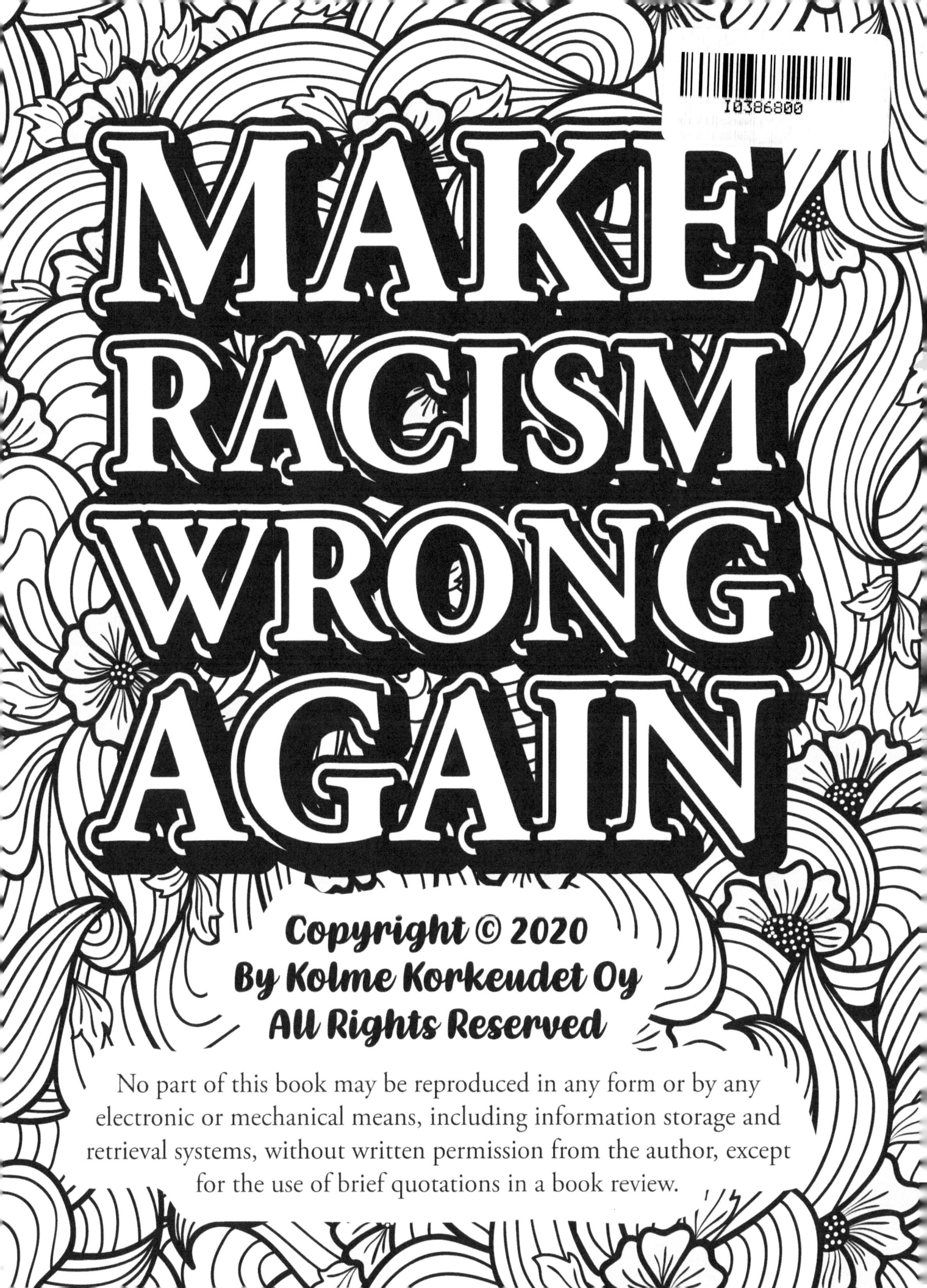“MAKE RACISM WRONG AGAIN

Copyright © 2020
By Kolme Korkeudet Oy
All Rights Reserved

No part of this book may be reproduced in any form or by any electronic or mechanical means, including information storage and retrieval systems, without written permission from the author, except for the use of brief quotations in a book review.

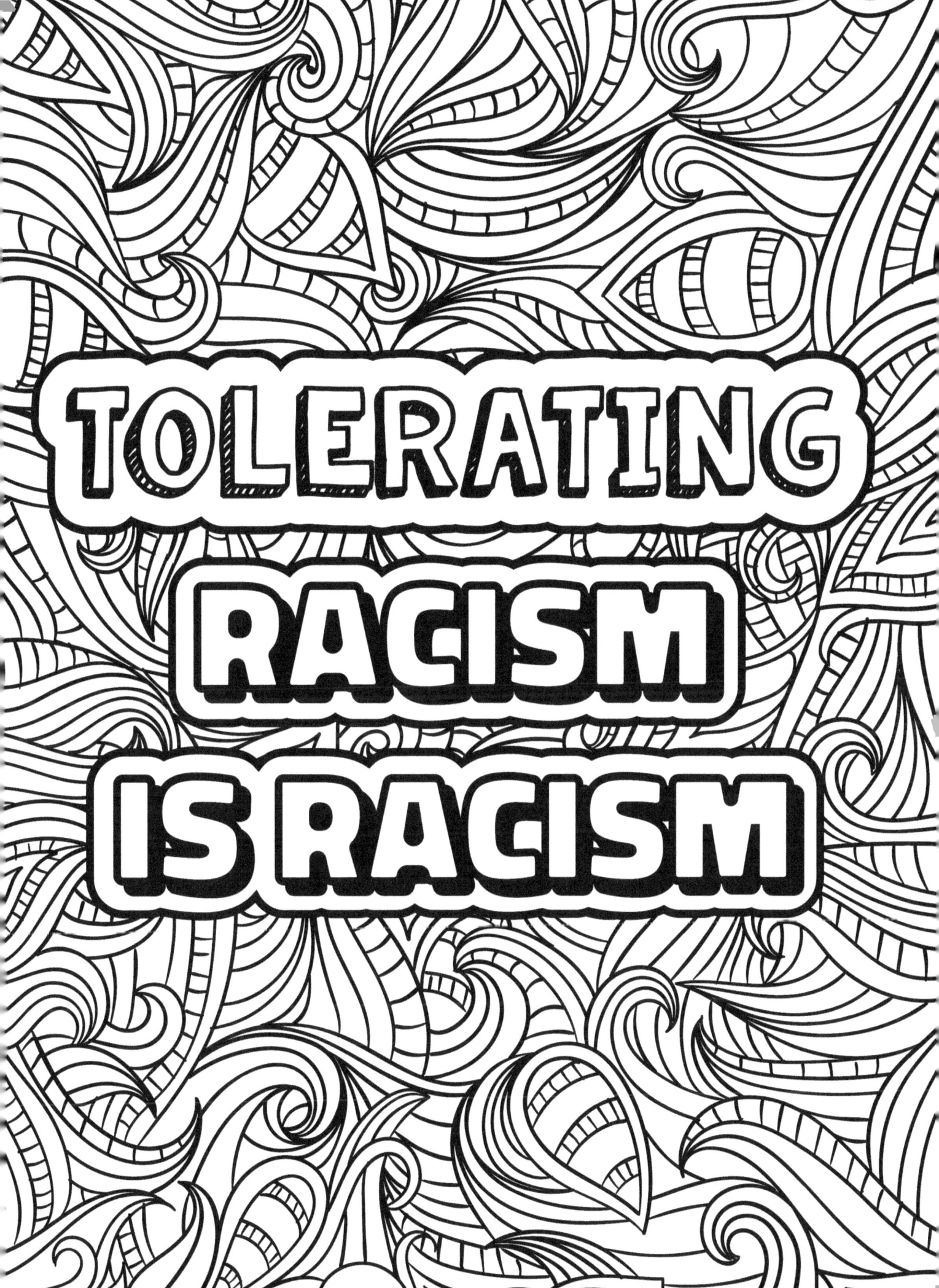

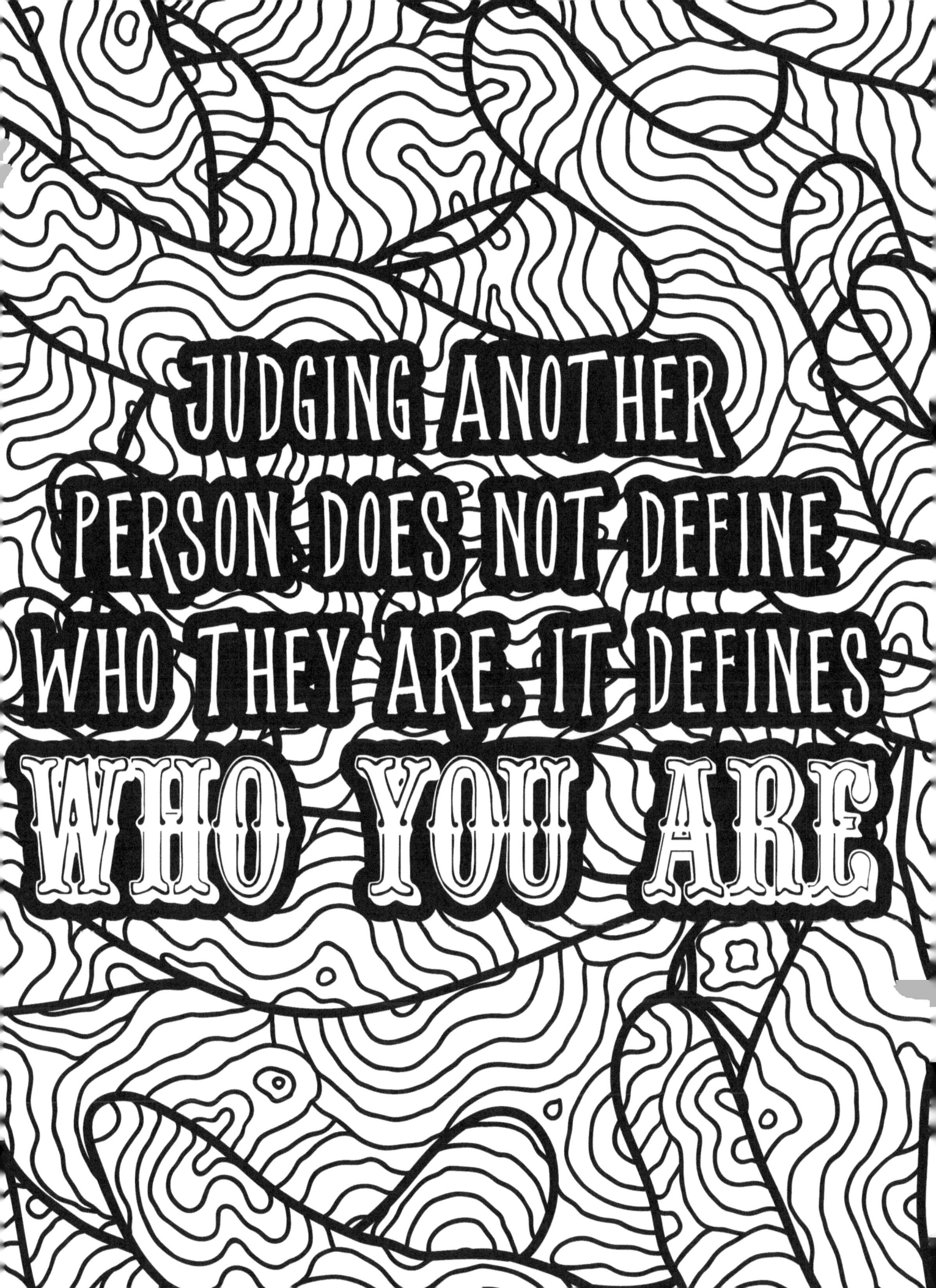

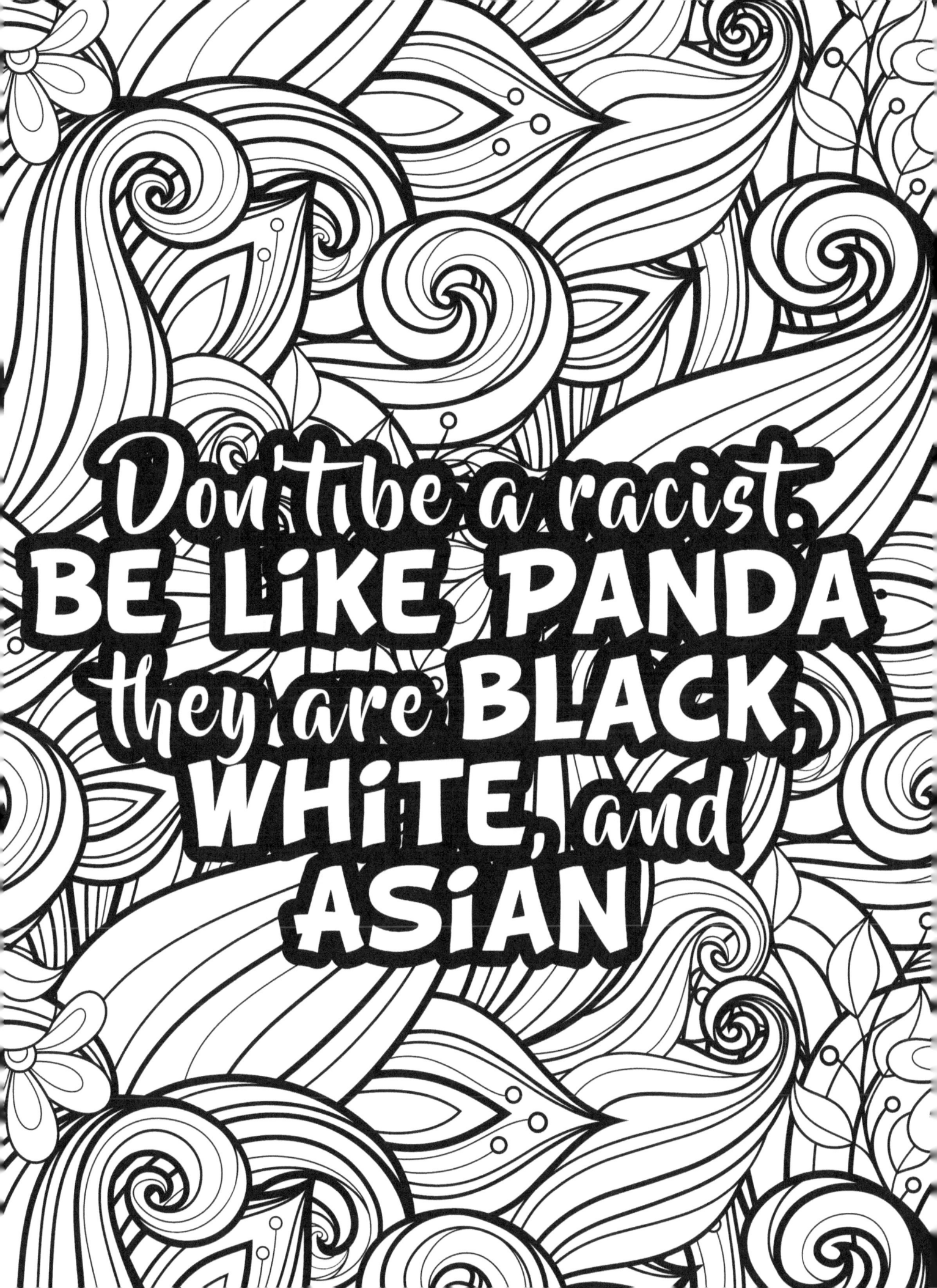

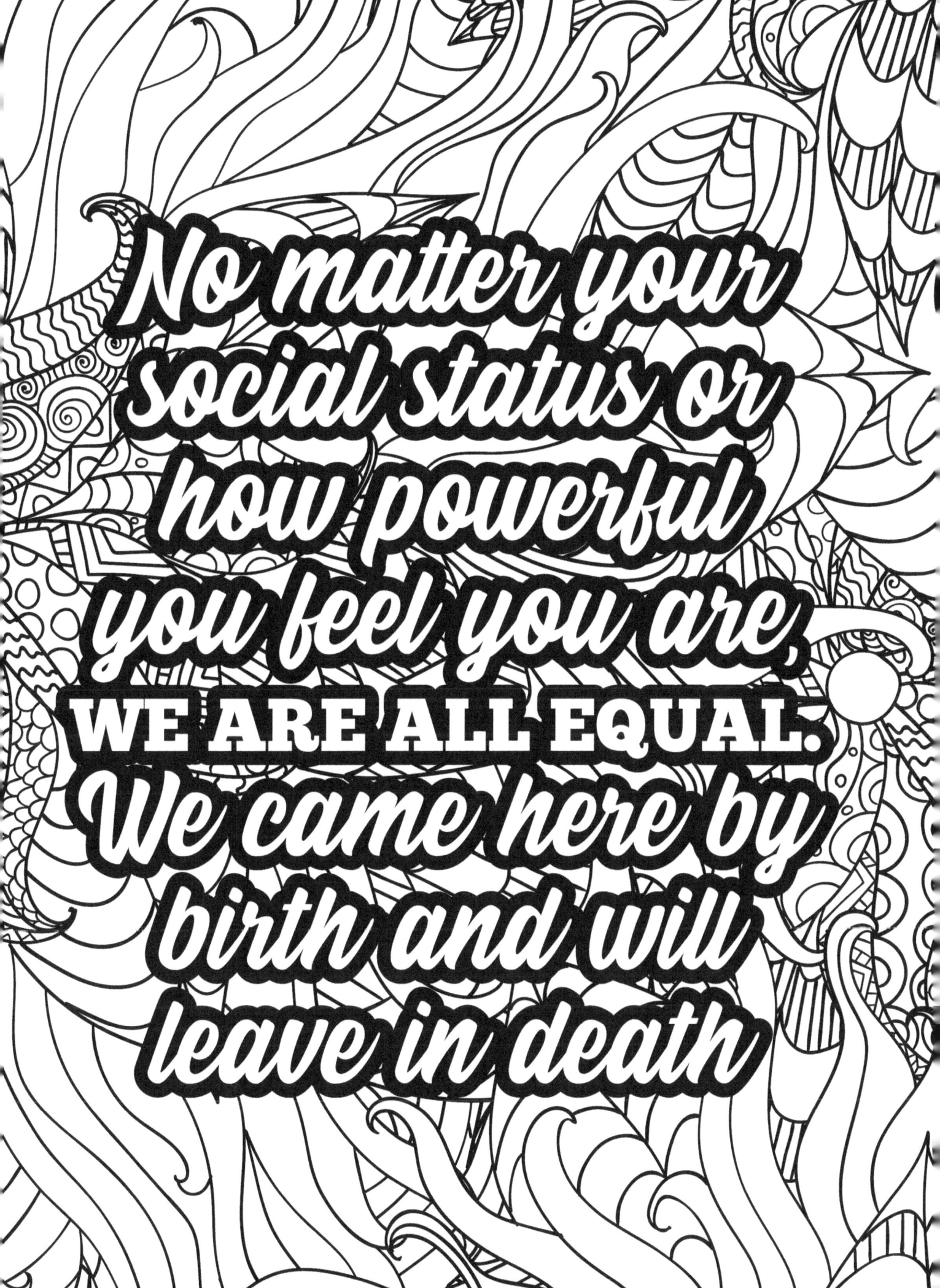

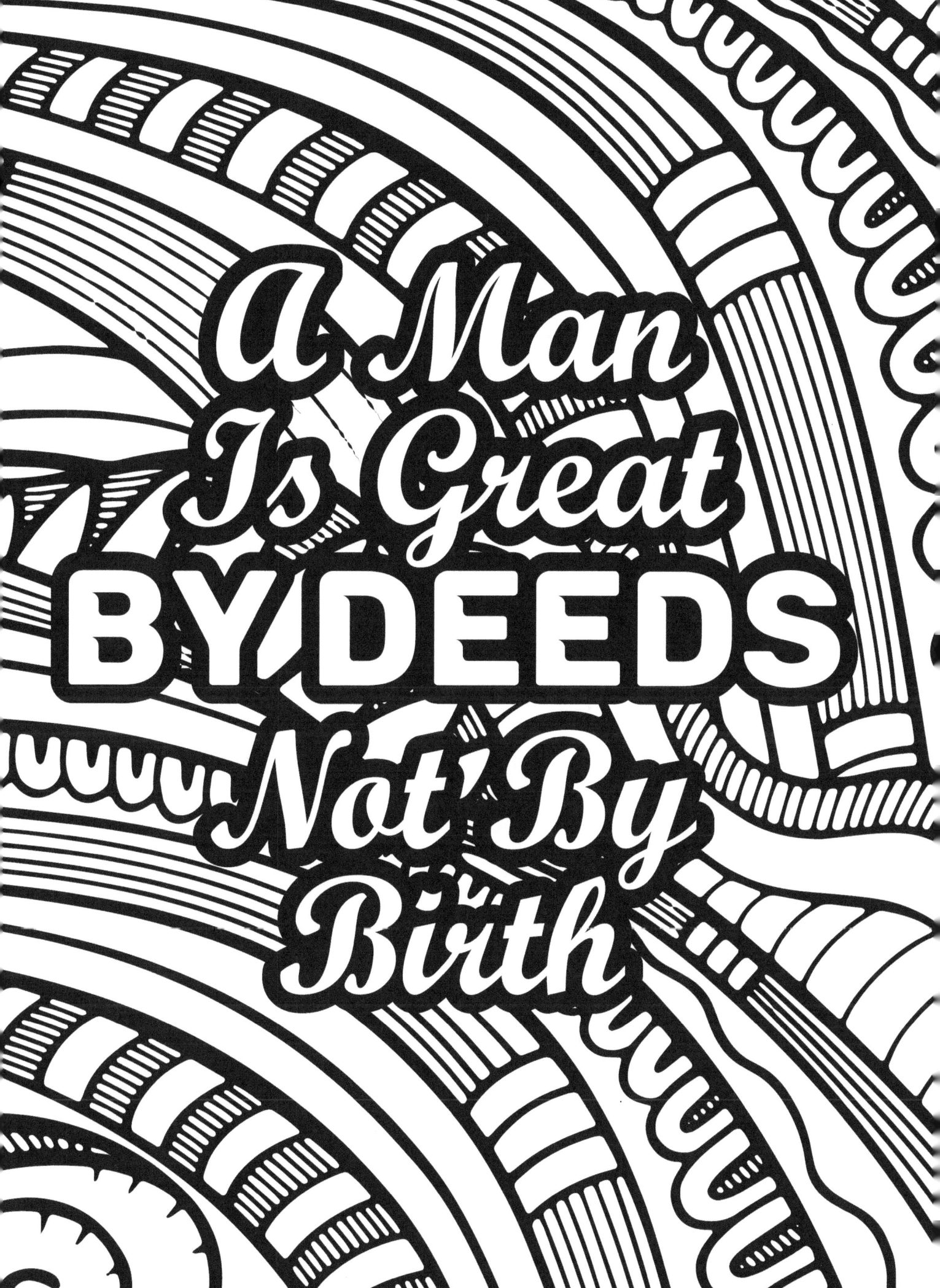

www.ingramcontent.com/pod-product-compliance
Lightning Source LLC
Chambersburg PA
CBHW080037120526
44589CB00037B/2713